Travelling
THROUGH THE ANCIENT STONES

A Collection of Illustrated Poems

GEORGE S. J. ANDERSON

STRATTON PRESS
We Celebrate Your Story

TRAVELLING THROUGH THE ANCIENT STONES
Copyright © 2023 **George S. J. Anderson**

Stratton Press Publishing
831 N Tatnall Street Suite M #188,
Wilmington, DE 19801
www.stratton-press.com
1-888-323-7009

ISBN (Paperback): 979-8-88764-426-4
ISBN (Ebook): 979-8-88764-466-0

Printed in the United States of America

Dedicated to those who still believe
poetry exists as a living entity
that changes lives
and breathes love and hope
into their souls…

Contents

Preface

Expressing my thoughts and feelings through poetry has been part of my life since age fourteen. Quite ill as a child, I suffered with uncontrolled asthma and was often isolated from friends and schoolmates. Sheltered in a clean room at age seven was a requirement my physicians mandated to keep me alive. The isolation enabled me to read the classics, which I consumed voraciously. By the time I was twelve, I had an appetite for Dumas, Poe, Twain, Wells, Verne, Dostoyevsky, and many writers of classical literature. In their writings, I found a context of human nature and hope for humanity I would not have found elsewhere. While my friends learned to play football and baseball, I learned the great life lessons of Chekov, Stevenson, Shakespeare, Dickens, and many others.

At fourteen, my English instructor encouraged me to start writing my thoughts in a journal. Her encouragement began after she read a short story I had written for her class assignment. It wasn't my story that interested her, but a short poem I had written in it. "That," she told me as she pointed to the poem, "is what you ought to be writing."

I took her advice and continued to write poetry until this very day, well over fifty years later.

Over the years, many of these poems were included in various collections. Some poems were illustrated in two publications of my book *Seasons in Cancer*. The first publication of *Seasons in Cancer* was in 2000, which contained eleven illustrations. In the 2022 edition, I continued with refining the text and did an additional twenty illustrations. I have always wanted to illustrate my poetry, but I needed to have the time and insight before I made the attempt. Through these pages, the drawings interpreted within this collection of poetry will show you the visions I had when I wrote these verses over my lifetime.

Now as the lights burn low, I wanted to fulfill a lifelong dream to publish these poems with meaningful artwork. I never had an opportunity to participate in formal art courses but took it upon myself to study and learn something about it on my own.

As the ardent glow fades from these final burning embers, a raw rudimentary understanding of mediums beyond the lead pencils I commonly used for years has become part of my palate. Now, with pastels, ink, charcoal, acrylics, and other media, I incorporated inspired drawings with my poetry to reference insights traced behind the emotions that fashioned them. Come with me as we begin *Travelling Through the Ancient Stones*…

George S. J. Anderson

Untitled #1

Untitled # 1

I hold these ashes in my hands
The raging fire in my veins
Runs from the ruined temple of my soul
My thoughts wandering there
Like the hauntings of a ghost...

My words are on fire
No papyrus can hold them
They burn in the evening sky
Like an effigy to the dying sun...

I am a lion
And I am afraid
There are wounds written
Into the lines of my poetry...

In the dying light
We kissed each other
In our underwear.
We ran to a hill beneath a
Nocturnal sky
And counted the stars.

In the light we tore each other's hearts to pieces
Looking for the soul hidden behind them.
With tear-spun threads
With needles wrought of patience and love
We mended them using pieces of each other...

When we were complete
We kissed each other
Clothed in our
Immaculate nakedness...

In darkness we walked
Hand in hand to a hilltop.
We stood in awe, marveling at
The infinite starlight...

Within my words still burning the horizon
Morning struggled another day
You are here still beside me
I am here in your embrace...

Untitled #1

As many of these poems remain untitled, *Untitled #1* was the first of many written after my wife died from breast cancer. We were married a little over thirty-four years when she died in early 2011. The aftermath of not rejoining the world when she passed was depressing. Even more disturbing was the difficulty of finding a companion to share the remainder of my life with. It seemed such a contentious ambition based on what I experienced trying to date again in later life.

Untitled #1 is an actualization of what I hoped I'd find in a relationship following the devastating loss of my wife. The first verses of the poem are definitive of the hollowness I was feeling at the time. The subsequent stanzas are descriptive of our flawed human condition as it is, revealing an intimate progression of shared experiences of having lived.

In the dying light
We kissed each other
In our underwear.

We ran to a hill beneath a
Nocturnal sky
And counted the stars…

I found this stanza particularly significant as it tells we would not be afraid to expose ourselves to new experiences, letting our proverbial "guard" down.

Near the end of the poem, the concept created in this stanza is then completed as the following defines the depth of its summation.

> In darkness we walked
> Hand in hand to a hilltop.
> We stood in awe, marveling at
> The infinite starlight...

This defines the poem. No longer are we counting the stars, but we are marveling at the universe above us. It has become a relationship that is shared and has more meaning and depth than when it first started. And to that end, there is struggle and sometimes pain to achieve it.

The illustration I created for this one was symbolized with multicolored tiles leading up to an inscribed heart where the two figures embrace. This symbolizes the pieces put together to unify them. The bodies are the colors of a sunset rising within them, and the remainder of the drawing shows symbols written into the poem.

January

January

They say you were superstitious
In your youth
In stride…with vigor
You are lost in time…
Stinging with the pain of years
Walking on…thinking of the ways
That you may have passed by
In your quest for simplicity…
Fingers burned on pages
Turning…
Some may remember you
Standing in their doorways.
While outside
Looking through panes
With flat glass-colored windows
You might have been there.
Peculiar it seems
With the hourglass on its side
The hands pale
The throngs of madness
Burning the night
With vicious letters
Ascribing them to you.
The houses I found wandering…
The places where I dwelled…
The soul I must seize…
The body I must leave in time…
Watches unknowing.
Remorse feeling no sorrow
Walking through ashes

Black and cold as winter
And the throng in rhapsody
Weaves in and out these
Empty sidewalks
Looking for themselves.
World convulsing on a course
Around the sun
And no one listens…
The horde of astral travelers
Walks to the edge of sanity
During a total eclipse of the sun
While they burn the witches
Before them
In the mirrors
They buy…
When in my youth
I once called them superstitious…

January

"January" is one of those poems that need something to define it, which is the word *time*. I chose the title "January" as it is the month in any given year where "time" begins, either figuratively or literally.

> They say you were superstitious
> In your youth
> In stride. With vigor
> You are lost in time…

We never knew when time began, so in a way, it is a kind of superstition as to why it began or why it exists. Time is lost into and beyond itself, though its "stride" remains vigorous and constant. So many things in our lives get counted like "pages burning" or an "hourglass" momentarily on its side before it is turned completely over again. And it "is" up to us to find some meaning in the passage of the times in which we live, while there are others who find nothing or curse the concept of time while trying to find meaning in it. Some will find meaning, and some will hate the existence in which they find themselves.

> The horde of astral travelers
> Walks to the edge of sanity
> During a total eclipse of the sun
> While they burn the witches

Before them
In the mirrors
They buy...

The illustration was difficult to create as the poem's theme is abstract. Somehow I needed to convey the idea there was something "mysterious and superstitious" occurring within the drawing. To build this atmosphere, I decided to create an abandoned village (at what looks like night, though actually, it is an eclipse of the sun) positioned in the unnatural shadows. In this darkness are hooded figures making their way into ruins of an old church. I felt this utilized an avenue to create the theme of superstition. The hourglass on its side was directly taken from the poem and becomes the pretense "that all is not what it seems to be." I created the foundation of *January* as winter themes since the month exists within this time, which finally led me to the finished work.

The Reasons

The Reasons

When the pen touches paper
The world spins...
The days slip by
One by one
Carelessly living all these spent moments
That lay with the rest.

In this moment, a certain madness exists
Here in this room...
The words become a mist
For something
I can't quite recall.

A fire envisioned inside me.
This rushing inferno blazing
Behind these eyes.
Unquenchable until
The lines appear
In a discordant melody
Only I hear...

The pen crawls over
The eternal pages
And one by one
The ink from the stylus
Becomes some strange
Apparition against my hand.

Ghosts and phantoms
Crawl in and out
The pores of a heart.
Finding blood of fire and ice
Melting in words
Transforming the story
Of written flames behind these eyes…

A sigh harbored
Against the corners of my mouth
Falls silently like whispers in a mist
Perhaps a tear may linger there
On the shuttered
Windowpanes…

I close the door to this tangled place…
It's just a dusty mansion…
Until I open the doors
Where I wander again
And find a part of me
I left inside…

The Reasons

"The Reasons" is a poem about why we write. Haunted by thoughts, devoured by a need to be written out as uneven glyphs on papyrus, words scribble out their purity in sentences designed of ink and paper. I wrote this one to explain what the process is like for me.

There are times when we write to express feelings, injustices, or life's strange ironies surfacing like moments of epiphanies as we chronicle the insights of our daily lives. I think it is a way to connect with others, and sometimes, it is a way to connect with myself.

> I close the door to this tangled place…
> It's just a dusty mansion…
> Until I open the doors
> Where I wander again
> And find a part of me
> I left inside…

I conceived this illustration where a "dusty mansion" appeared like a "haunted house" as seen through the safety of the subject's window. The desk, surrounded by books and papers, becomes the "safe haven" from where he/she attempts to find comfort from their ever-present thoughts. I left the foreground of the illustration partially undone, symbolizing work that will never be completed! When you write, it is an undertaking (possibly an obsession/curse) that never finds any conclusions.

Untitled #2

Untitled #2

If I was the rain
I would open you up
Like the blossoms of a prairie field...

If I was the sun
I would touch your naked skin in warm light
You could feel down inside your soul...

If I was the moon
I would spin a silver web of light
To catch beautiful dreams for you to sleep in peace...

If I was the wind
I would tousle your hair, kiss your cheeks,
And dance with you beneath the blowing leaves...

If I were the stars
I would fall like diamonds to lie at your feet
Like a crystal path for you to follow home...

But I am just a man with dreams
Of rain and sun, the moon, wind, and stars
With only arms open to hold you,

Kisses to caress you
And these words so lowly said
To win your precious heart....

Untitled #2

"Untitled #2" has a predictable theme about the dream we all have about finding love. I wrote this one day as intuitive imaginings of what I would say if I ever found someone to share my remaining life's adventures.

The poem was particularly difficult to illustrate as I needed to incorporate different times throughout a day in one drawing. In doing this, I created a landscape of the sun and moon and then dissected them with a bolt of lightning. After deciding how to design the sky, I simply contained the rest of the elements of the poem and placed them into the foreground.

The drawing was dominantly created with pencil tracing under pastels. It was the first time I attempted to use acrylics to heighten colors. However, the overplay of acrylics in this particular drawing revealed my beginner's inexperience with the medium. In spite of my inexpert workmanship, the design seemed to work. I used silver ink to brighten stars, which I needed as a path of stars passing beyond the subject in the foreground. It was, in my opinion, a little overachieved, yet effective for the illustration! Overall, it was not my best creation, but the outcome was what I had aimed for.

Journeys

Journeys

We've been through the shapes of change
And we shake off the dust of the journey
Come with me and share
The breath of my living
In an instant we can sail
To the horizon
With the sails of all the answers
That lie in whispers
Beneath the pillows of sleep
With all our dreams
To guide us
We'll map a course
That we'll follow
With our waking
And we'll not
Let a moment
Slip by our eyes
And we'll shake off the dust
Of yesterday
And share the breath of changing
On our passage
Through time

Journeys

I wrote "Journeys" for my late wife in 1977. Not having much money back then, I presented it to her as a gift for one of those special occasions. The poem was intended to illustrate the truth of any relationship, which is we don't always know what is coming at us from the next corner, the next journey. However, standing together, we always will find a way to surmount it, growing together as we do.

So as the poem is about transition, I knew I needed to create an illustration to demonstrate that very thing. In the illustration, you will notice numerous transitions. The one side of the picture shows flowers and foliage while the other side is rocks and hillsides. Even the butterflies are transitioning from orange-brown to a blue-green as they fly over the dreamer toward the ever-changing sea. There are many other concepts of transition in the drawing, but I'll leave it up to you to see them.

The drawing took several long days and nights to complete. It is a collaboration of ink and dry pastels intricately woven together to show transitions from one state of being to another. The execution of this illustration had to be exact in its placement of subjects to allow the flow of concepts throughout the drawing.

Daydream Life

Daydream Life

When you were younger
Remember how your elders would say
That you'd do so much better
Than they ever did
Then you had your whole
Life to live
Now you are older
Trying to be wiser
Never did build your
Palaces in the clouds
And you sit here thinking
About when you get started
How things will be
Thinking you are wiser
You stare out a window
In
A
Dream

Daydream Life

This is a poem about dreaming your life instead of living it. I think many of us do this from time to time. It actually becomes a problem if all we do is dream. For in these dreams, we trap ourselves (our spirits) in a prison (a tower) from which we may never escape.

To illustrate this idea, I created a dream world beyond a tower where the shadow of a figure looks out from his barred windows. His dream lies beyond the confines of the tower where he watches his dreams play out before him.

The drawing is almost exclusively created with pastels and a minimum of inking to draw out some of the details.

Illusions

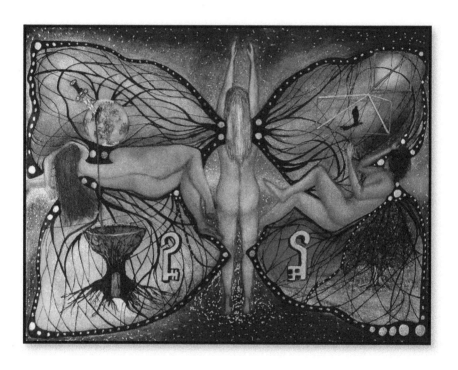

Illusions

Obscured by reason
Comes the hazy season
Challenging butterflies
Before the illusion
Disintegrates in the
Azure ionosphere

Vision is not seeing
Blue rainbows span across
The fields of imagination
Geometrical perpendicular
World sliced by bitter knives
Drink in the wind
Taste the wine

Heard the fine breaking of tears
The rainfall of mystery
Miraged into the silence
Engaged in the coffee night…
Light falls on its drunken face
Just to start something new
Laughing is just about the way it is
No way is the right way
Especially if it's yours

Dormant answers lie in cellar closets
The questions can't find the key
Just looking around the corner
See if you can buy me one
It only costs your life
If you haven't got one
You can get anything you like

Whatever happened to yesterday?
Did you find
It was really in your hands
A moment ago?
Obscured by reason
The hazy season
Butterflies
Are just an illusion…

Illusions

"Illusions" was written in the early 1980s. It was the time when AIDS became part of our vocabulary. When this disease was discovered coming into our country, the government did very little to recognize it as a threat. It was only when women and children started to become infected and dying that an outcry went out, causing intense investigation and eventual treatment. The effect it had on our trust of the government to protect us was severely damaged. I believe this was the core of the poem "Illusions," a "world sliced by bitter knives," and "It only costs your life…If you haven't got one… You can get anything you like…"

Since 2019 and beyond, the world suffered with a much deadlier disease…coronavirus! The same thing happened, as it did in the 1980s, and many people died. Here is something I wrote for my friend who lost her mother to COVID-19.

Love Letter from Air

Do not judge God for times like these. These are times when the world is filled with intelligent lies. Our children sing hymns to the apocalypse while our dirge of sad eulogies fills our mouths with sorrow and blame. We've abandoned hope to the bottom of a wishing well while others wait patiently for the tiger to take away their pain. The pews are empty as we walk away in the narrows single-file without a glimpse or touch from anyone. It is sometimes, in the quiet moments, in the stalled glimmers of despair, when we truly learn to breathe. And I can feel its emptiness…like air.

The earth will stay as it belongs… Soil, stone, and mountains will remain agelessly as they did in days before. The water will move freely, bordered only by lands and kingdoms of ice. Fire is limited only by what it can consume. Only air can be everywhere, at all times, over everything corporeal, possessing an integrity and relativity of its own nature. It whispers in the quiet, with a voice too low to hear, "In silence is affirmation." Bearing the winds of change, we cling as best as we can to what we hold dear.

I dreamed of rain…falling with a kind of violence that would eventually become peaceful, wondering if my melancholy breathed such dreams in wakeful hours. In such fevered dreams, eloquent words walked away, disappearing into blurred shadows against the fog. In the gloaming, I felt empty…like air.

Upon what passions have we built our lives, and what grave burdens have paled the colors of our grace? Yet it is what life brings us, not what we imagine it should be, that its final offerings gives us moments to pause…to breathe. Break conviction with the perceptions of truth we hold. Make them offerings to the darkness for we must despair the truth, for only God knows it. Integrity, spinning itself into cracks of light before the dawn, should lead us beyond the naked confusion found within a starless night. Aware of my hallowed spirit, I feel empty…like air.

Dreams wander these endless corridors of hope, peering inside open doors, never satisfying its wanderlust of endless domains. Dreams hunt in fertile fields of imagination for ripened aspiration and then demands "passion" harvest ambitions from it as living treasure. Conviction gathers ambitions in parceled clay pots of worthiness. There they wait impatiently…where time will either nurture or destroy them. Every earthen vessel exhausts their importance as passion dies. Time discards every one. In broken shards, outdated with insignificance, the remnants of spirits unfurl as their seasons fade to air. A haunted air, bountiful with broken terra-cotta memories, fills the endless emptiness with failing voices. The antecedent of despair, ambition fragments with decay. Prophesies foretold with broken frailty end every dim epiphany in cruel twilight. Somehow the still-lingering fragrance of living treasures endures despite all judgment. Clothed in the residual quiet, I feel empty…like air.

Ambition, fostering my career as a registered nurse, faded to obscurity as forty-two years disappeared in memories both cherished and wounded. Crippling pain of my mortality were wounds with deep memories. It is regret, and it is hope, teetering on the threshold of belief that brought me here. The destination always had directions, but there were never any signs to mark the way. Did we live in the sweat of a compassionate fire, or was it a moment of madness when we aspired to be more than our ambitions?

We once had warrior hearts spending the last heat of daylight when the mêlée broke into our ranks. Insidious and mysterious, the realization of an invader in our midst, coming without a name, advancing on faces lying in our wards, garnered death and suffering on those we swore to protect. In retaliation, we brought paper gowns, hooded masks with visors, and doubled gloves as weapons against an unknown aggressor. Superiors and governing powers mocked us when we asked for the name of our enemy and then told us to go about our work as if no threat existed. We gathered courage behind our paper defenses, counted the corpses taken from our wards, and prayed for ourselves and the countless many affected by this faceless adversary.

Prayers are not for the chaste but for the wounded, and there were many. It was a very long time before it was given a name… AIDS—a blood-borne pathogen. In its wake of dead, the governing powers deigned it as a threat, something my fellow warriors and colleagues knew from the beginning.

It is now when I have retreated from the ranks of my fellow warriors that I feel I have abandoned them. To be left behind feels more like mercy than the injuries dealt by the age I have become. I watch in reverence as my compassionate warriors cast tears at unseen specters and walk through a gauntlet of ghosts with courageous hearts. I feel empathy for them for as they wage many battles one at a time in the war of lives, the governing powers mock them and degrade the lost dead with insignificance. No longer can I walk the steps of my companions for I would be more burden than support. No longer can I give you the labor of my hands, so I offer you the solace of my heart.

I dreamed of snow…falling with a gentleness that would eventually become violent, burying a cacophony of lies and hateful noise, wondering if melancholy breathed such dreams in the darkest hours. I breathed into the cold air, watching my breath become a white mist against the falling snow. With a wounded prayer, I set my heart upon the air. Carried to all wherevers and whenevers, every dark corner, every suffered heart, it exists in whatever dream you find it. If you ever need the solace of a compassionate heart, I set it upon the air. I feel the air, and it is all around me…just breathe.

With love,
Air

"Illusions" had to be illustrated in a way that was a bit ominous yet beautiful to look at. Using the idea that one life succeeds over another's failure was something I wanted to establish as the primary *illusion*, creating what seems to be one entity from two fallen ones. Seeing the two fallen beings absorbed into one individual is unnerving. Again, taking context from the poem, the concept of "butterflies are just an illusion" set the palate for what became the illustration. Even now, I feel the picture resonating in a discomforting way every time I look at it.

Portrait of the Universe

Portrait of the Universe

There were days I could have laughed
But didn't…
There were days I could have cried
But couldn't…
There were days I should have said
But words passed them by.
There were years that were
But then they lost their time.
There were tears that should have fallen
But eyes remained too dry.
Then there were the times of vision
But no one could see…
Yet all I could do
Was take my brush
And with my single color
Paint the world.
Hoping to add to
The portrait of the universe
A color it might be missing
If not touched
By my hand…

Portrait of the Universe

This poem essentially asks, "What is my worth?" The answer is life would be less rich without contributions from everyone existing in this time. We are all colors, and each of us has a contribution of brushstrokes to paint on this portrait. Imagine a world without colors. Imagine how drab and uninspiring it would be. We are here…in this place…in this time…only once before it all fades away. Only the words of our journey here will remain…in our memories…in our hearts…for as long as there is one of us to remember.

But how do you make a portrait of the universe? What really defines a portrait? It is my opinion the eyes define the many portraits I have seen throughout my lifetime. So using this concept, I created an eye connected to both the atmosphere above and the earth beneath. I made the bond between the eye and the earth as tears falling like a waterfall and as a corona extending colored rays above as a link to the infinite heavens.

The drawing is made predominately of dry pastels. After creating the context of the illustration (which is the eye, the corona, and the firmament beneath), the upper half of the picture seemed naked. To remedy this, I decided to create a kind of calligraphy border to give the work a sense of definition. Unlike the rest of the drawing, this border was made of inks and acrylics as it needed to be imprinted on a drawing already treated with a fixative.

The Cage

The Cage

What is life my friends?
I once thought it over
And the answers were few.
Is it a brief interlude?
A sanctuary in the path of eternity?
Or is it a struggling mass
Of bodies in a bleak sweating cage
Looking for the steel door
That brought them here?
All I know
Is when I walked
I learned of others,
Finding them much like myself…
Struggling to be free…
But in this struggle
I found someone
To share this life…
Transcending now to happiness
I am alive…
The steel doors
Do not matter anymore…
I am only put here
To learn…
And know sharing …
Is all I ever have
To give…
As will my life be…
Through all eternity

The Cage

This is a poem I wrote in 1974, which received international recognition. It speaks to answer why are we here, and what investiture are we to make while we exist? I never felt it was one of my better poems, but then, I am my own worst critic.

When considering how I wanted to illustrate this topic, I studied what other artists considered cages (or prisons) to look like. As a very general description, I found various areas of confinement with walls, steel bars, hazardous bulwarks of razor wires, and towering stockades made of rocks and mortar. Nothing I found really gave me a sense of the kind of prison I envisioned when I wrote this poem. So I continued with the concept of isolation and solitude, evaluating what other artists conceived these concepts to be in various forms of art. Nothing I found fit the concepts I was tying to visualize. Eventually, I just started drawing what I felt about the drawing and answered the question, "What kind of place would become a 'prison' without exploiting the traditional concepts of walls, wire, and steel bars?" This drawing is my answer to that question.

This drawing is exclusively created with pastels and drawing pencils. Blending the pastels to create the dimensions of shadows was the greatest challenge I had with this one. Creating this landscape ultimately designed itself into the area of confinement I envisioned with steep unsurmountable cliffs and ledges. It is an inescapable enviorment. Yet as the two figures on the cliff realize, the discovery of being together has the spirtual power to escape the grip of their surroundings.

Harvesting Time

Harvesting Time

The time of the harvesting arrives
On the death throes of winter
Snow is piled high
Like sheaves of pale wheat
The workings of the plough man
Trees burgeon
Beneath their whitened burden
While footsteps
In the garden
Turn brown in earthen colors
Alive…crawling through
With the promise of flowers
This baptism of white melting
Away from this ancient font…
Prayers of intercession
Murmuring, in whispers,
As the earth removes
Its whitened mantle
To birth the child
From its pregnant soil…

Harvesting Time

Generally, we believe the time of harvest arrives in autumn when all the summer produce is stocked away as canned or jarred goods while the barns are filled with bales of clover, hay, summer wheat, barley, and rye. My sense of harvesting time turns snow into sheaves while any naked ground foretells the beginnings of new growth and hope. In a way, we harvest these signs of life into our hearts as winter melts away and hope for new beginnings to arrive.

The old deities of forgotten folklore were often depicted as beings that controlled earth's nature, clothed in skins of men and women, constantly fighting and undermining each other to maintain their status. In this drawing, I depicted Spring as a female entity with her eyes closed, but with a certainty when they opened, the world would flourish in bright flowers and life. Winter, also depicted in a female entity, has her eyes closed in sleep as she knows and accepts her reign coming to an end.

I worked this drawing from a pencil sketch and then placed dry pastels over the underlying format. Blending the colors with the dark lead helped create shadows where I wanted them. After colors were applied and blended, I redid the background with colored pastel pencils to give it definition. Acrylics were utilized to heighten the colors of the flowers just below the depiction of spring.

Old Friends

Old Friends

And so, old friend
The time of our parting
Is at hand
The path we travel
Parts here at this pass
This new road I travel
Has a cause
Much different from yours
So as friends we pass
To be old friends
Parting hands
Finding new ones
To plant in our hearts
Time tolls the bells
Of our keeping
Waking desires
Soft the dreams
While we are sleeping
We have new beginnings
Wrought of flesh and bone
So that we might find new friends
On the tightropes of life
And by chance we may meet again
Old friends
With hopes and desires
While making new friends
Till we make them old friends
As you and I
Must now pass...

Old Friends

"Old Friends" is a poem I wrote about forty years ago and has been published many times over the years. I included it in *Seasons in Cancer* and in numerous poetry collections. It is one of those poems I wished to illustrate to the best of my ability and would be inherently expressive of its meaning.

As I went about creating this work, I wanted to include elements of the poem, such as two friends parting ways to move on to other destinations in their lives. This was especially challenging considering the media I needed to utilize to get the idea across. I thought of the many models I could use, like two men parting ways at a diverging path, but this thought might be misconstrued to mean something darker. Then again, the thought of two women embracing at the diverging path would be misinterpreted as well. A man and a woman parting ways at the path could mean something entirely dissimilar than the point I was trying to make. It was very frustrating.

It wasn't until I explained the problem to my girlfriend that she simply said, "Just draw two children walking up the path together." It was a brilliant idea. I just wasn't thinking on that level! I decided to do that very thing and get started. After all, being "friends" is a gesture of innocence and vulnerability, is it not? Even Stephen King once said, "I never had any friends later on like the ones I had when I was 12—Jesus, did you?"

Ah, but the story does not end there! When I draw, I like to have a model of some type to work from. Even in my innumerable art books on figure and anatomy profiles, there is not one illustration of the entire body of a child, much less the figures of two children walking together. I could get the head and shoulders as models, but perhaps for two young boys or two little girls walking together, I had to go to the Internet. To say there was a bit of concern and discomfort searching for such illustrations would be putting it mildly. As I explored the Internet sites for an appropriate rendering, I kept wondering if my front door would be kicked in as I searched. Not kidding!

Eventually, after searching for hours, I found only two pictures I felt would work in my application. I utilized elements of both. Though I generally like three or more pictures to work from, two models had to do!

When I finished the completed work, I pondered the significance of the quest. There were many essential elements missing from a world I once believed to be good and wholesome. Now, it seemed to be steered with skepticism and hypocrisy, which transcended into unimaginable foulness.

My memories of "friends" are filled with good feelings, laughter, and comradery. Such illustrations of my embraces, handshakes, hugs, and kisses with friends and family could certainly be twisted into less-innocent interpretations by those with no right to judge us. My idyllic memory of children playing, or walking together down a dusty autumn road, or two boys watching trout swim from warm summer banks of a stream are images fading to extinction. I simply wondered, as I finished the drawing, where our dream went. Were we sleeping, or were we awake…when it wandered away?

The Hour of the Child

The Hour of the Child

Mother, lay down your apron
And leave the pot on the stove
Let the world here that surrounds us
Sit on the windowsill with the rose
Let the breeze blow a song around us
For his time is nearly come
This hour of life storms upon us
With the eloquent laughter of a child
He is a moment of an hour
A discordant note of song
Bejeweled with eyes of sapphire light
Aglow with the face of the sun
He plays games of twenty questions
And all my answers are ten too few
He asks me of God, and I tell him the sky
Is His window and the clouds are His beard
As he gives in to a moment of sleep
I watch as his hour slips away
Oh please, put down your chores, dear Mother
For this child's soon a man, but for now
Let him dream his dreams
Beneath the blanket of sleep
On the wake
Of the apple-blossomed ground…

The Hour of the Child

I had to make do with what I could find for a sleeping child. The poem hints at enjoying children while they are still children…not to leave life's everyday common chores overtake this wondrous moment of childhood.

I wrote this poem in 1981, which was a year after my son was born. Every day I saw new awareness growing in this tiny person, and with it, I realized this moment was fading every day. Eventually, I would only have fond memories of his time as a child. I wrote this piece in memory of his childhood and for every mother and father watching their child growing day by day.

The drawing was drawn entirely with pencil and pastels. I incorporated most of the essentials in the poem onto the drawing. Seeing the mother watching from the kitchen window as her child sleeps peacefully beneath the limbs of a nearby apple tree was an essential metaphor I needed to create this illustration.

Anatomy Class

(Graffiti Written on the Walls of the Long White Corridor)

Anatomy Class

(Graffiti Written on the Walls of the Long White Corridor)

Frog legs pinned to the waxen slabs…
Remove the heart
Cardiac arrest
Running lactated ringers
Formaldehyde smells linger
Can't you cut it?

Go to the next table
Eyes dulled against the pillows
Death smells musty against me
The trapezius muscle of a cat
Cold rush to the emergency room
Boxes of sterile technique on the floor
Ace bandage pasted to the walls
Can you cut it?

Running through the long white corridors
Asepsis in a septic tank
Look in close with a microscope
Pathology report
Through the steel blue surgery doors
The empty tray of blackened wax waiting
Take this body to the morgue
Probably couldn't cut it…

The formaldehyde smell lingers there
Reading the invisible scriptures written where
They pinned frog legs to the waxen slab
The trapezius muscle of a cat
Looking through the microscopes
Haunted steps join your every pace
Looking behind to see ahead
On your walk down the long white corridors…
Did you cut it?

Anatomy Class
(Graffiti Written on the Walls
of the Long White Corridor)

This was a poem I wrote around the time I was in nursing school (1972–1975). One thing said about students not returning to subsequent semesters was the student was "cut" from the program because he or she didn't make it (for various reasons).

The concept of being "cut" had deeper meanings and consequences metaphorically for me than what reality dictated. Could any of us really "cut it"? Could anyone measure up to the irreproachable standards for either our current situation or possible future situation in life? Who can really make such a judgment call or receive it? From that perspective came the concept of "Anatomy Class (Graffiti Written on the Walls of the Long White Corridor)."

Constructing this illustration took a lot of study of perspective with many pictures of various dissections. Anatomically, I needed dissections of a human, a frog, and a cat. I found a good dissection of a human in *Gray's Anatomy* and several feline dissections online. Utilizing parts of both, I conjoined the two dissections to illustrate a point.

Subsequently, after gathering the dissections, I went into studying the ruins of war. In a way, war scenes were metaphorically similar to what went on in a medical facility. *Life* is at war with *death*… Nurses, doctors, and every medical professional existing in this world wields a sword of healing and mediation, hoping somehow we have a hand in making things better. However, all names are written on the walls of the long white corridor. In the end, we will all be "cut" because none of us can "cut it."

The Fly

The Fly

A buzzing of a fly in the kitchen
Where last night's dishes sit
On the table
A ghost lingers there
In a chair
Sitting by a window
Looking out into
A surrealistic scene
Of flaming volcanic
Eruptions and translucent
Wings on sceptered winds
Where reality does not visit with
Its purifying nectar
Footsteps in the bedroom
Echoing softly and sliding
Down slowly on the walls
Like shadows
Of what may have been
Part of some fond memory
There in that instant of waking
There in that last breath of sleep
I hold a familiar sound to ear
Then turn around; there is nothing
Just a buzzing in the kitchen

The Fly

"The Fly" is a poem about failed communication and the fall-out that eventually leaves us imprisoned inside our own desolate thoughts. Eventually, all we are left with are the failing echoes of the "buzzing in the kitchen."

The drawing was challenging. It was created using dry pastels and acrylics in the background to heighten the color. Getting the concept of a volcanic eruption dissipating was difficult as each time I used a fixative on the pastels, the colors would fade. Eventually I found a blend of acrylic paint that eliminated the fading I encountered. Putting the male and female entities into the window frame came from the intentions of the poem. Encasing them inside the branches signified the entrapment in which they found themselves still alive, but encumbered by their own doing.

Since the concept is rather abstract, it made the drawing all the more difficult to create. There were a few visuals I could draw from the poem, which included the dishes and the fly. Using only these two elements to create the story became a challenge. The illustration eventually drew itself after I started putting it all together. This was the result.

Business Hours

Business Hours

If you cannot own the man
Then you must own his mind
It's just good business sense
To keep it in the black
Don't you ever hesitate
To keep everything in line
Keep production going
Make sure his soul is mine…

Punch them in at time clocks
Put them all in rows
March them in like soldiers
Stamped with the company seal
This is how they'll become
The sacrificed society
For the eternal metal wheel
Don't hesitate to mock them
If one is so inclined
To show the least incentive
That they would own their mind

Please keep this thought
In your remembrance
Sow it in your hearts
During business times
If you cannot own the man
Then simply own his mind

Business Hours

"Business Hours" is a poem about our paid slavery, something we feel (but never speak about) when we endeavor to go to work every day. The rules of the land and common morality never penetrate the rules of the workplace. To keep our jobs, we are expected to ignore our humanity and freedom until the closing hour of our confinement. Everything keeps bureaucrats and the aristocracy at their pleasures, leaving most of us to find our lives scratching in the dust for sustenance.

As a kind of coda or a stretch to the consequences of living this way, I saw the future as sleek, clean, and with a certain kind of clutter-organized beauty in it. However, in it I also saw the decline of humanity as well. To create this environment, I chose to show two figures in the foreground made of gears and mechanizations, exemplifying the lack of soul replaced with the standards of *the eternal metal wheel.*

The drawing is made predominantly with pastels in the sky and parts of the foreground. The silhouettes of the man and woman were initially created with black pastels, but the color would not stay consistent with a fixative. As an alternative, I tried a black acrylic paint, which seemed to get the effect I wanted. Some of the buildings in the foreground are acrylic based while others are actually pastels. Overall, I achieved the effect I wanted.

Life in the "Nth" Degree

Life in the "Nth" Degree

Living on and on in metered time
Living in the time of the "Nth" degree
You cannot cut your fingers
Don't put your life on the line
All the madness is gone
So now you have the time
To go on living…
In the time of the "Nth" degree

You can always wash your car
But don't see how fast it goes
Don't ever climb that mountain
We made the rule this year
Ever since that time
There've been no injuries here
Sign here please
Please pay the man
This way if you go
You'll have the Family Plan
It's the way we will know
You're living life to the fullest
Living your life to the "Nth" degree

So please wipe your nose
It might be contagious
And keep yourself inside
We'll keep you isolated
With us the rules don't slide
Keeps our records clean
'Cause we're living our life
To the "Nth" degree
Keep things organized
We just wanted a way
To help you all survive

You can't walk near the oceans
The rivers are too deep
The canyons are far too wide
Haven't lost anyone yet
Since we keep them all inside
Living their lives to the "Nth" degree
We took away all the madness
So we could all go mad
Inside

Life in the "Nth" Degree

This is the last of what I consider my "industrial" poems. I named it "Life in the 'Nth' Degree." The intent of the title is everyone hopes they are striving to live in the most "superlative" way they possibly can. The poem was challenging to illustrate as I struggled with a number of studies before I ever attempted to draw it.

Since the poem has a singular voice dictating commands, it was very abstract and complicated to perceive it as a drawing. Essentially, the poem is devoid of any significant visuals! I started various sketches and worked several ideas trying to approach this one. It wasn't until I considered how this would appear in the context of hopelessness that I finally came up with an idea. Even my original ideas changed as I progressed to the finalized drawing. Originally, considering two figures surrounded by what appears to be an entrapping brushy tree seemed like a good idea. However, the drawing looked entirely empty and unfinished until I added two additional figures.

"Life in the 'Nth' Degree" is essentially a pencil and pastel drawing. There is a modified ink wash over the tree in the foreground, highlighted by remarking some of the bark with black and gray inks and then doing an over wash. The color scheme had to look haunting, so applying both green and yellow hues to the sky worked well for this one.

The concept behind the title is too often we opt on the side of caution and forget we are here to experience and learn. Many times, caution shrinks our life to such a degree; we fail to discover opportunities meant to enrich our lives and the lives around us! Sometimes these cautions become rules or laws we can never again encroach in our lifetime! Some of us may remember riding in the bed of a pickup truck as a kid and surviving it! I know I did! Try that one today... see how far it goes before consequences appear! *"We took away all the madness...So we could all go mad...Inside..."*

The Innkeeper

"There's a knocking at the door,"
Said the Innkeeper at his chore.
"Someone's calling in the wind.
                    Open the door and
Let him in."
Through the opened doorway
                    The face he saw
                                Could have been his own…
Could have been ten thousand
                    Common faces
He saw before.
"Let him by…"
                    The Innkeeper implored…
The door was opened
                    A haggard man stood there
Just outside…
The man looked about the barroom
Through the opened wood-hewn door…
                    Dazed inside a deadly sleep
He gasped out unattended words
                    A language he couldn't speak
                                Sentences collapsed in ruins
Into an exhausted heap
                    Then he fell…very still…
Lying on the barroom floor…
                    The customers swore,

"The man's a wretch
                The son of a whore."
The Innkeeper's eyes
                Were shining bright.
"Bring him upstairs…
                Lie him to bed
                        This night."
No one moved to help him
                When the Innkeeper plied his plight.
Everyone amusedly clamored…
                The pints of ale poured round…
On every skeptic's face…
                They painted their own
                        Self-fabricated frowns…
Foaming whiskers, swilling frothy pints
                They just kept going down.

No assistance was forthcoming
                    So he did the best he could
Got beneath his shoulders
                    As the man then groaned, half stood...
Then walked him to a vacant room
                    And laid him on the bed.
Stayed a moment looking down...
                    Then said a prayer
                        Made of whispers there
                            Meant only for the dead...
The stars outside
                    Were scattered gleamings...
Captured moments, becoming aspects of light
That once upon danced on fairies' wings
                    Now roaming the skies at night.
                    Fashioned lead-cased windows held
The choreograph of colored glass glowing
                    Rubbed into imprisoned radiance
                        By points of ruby
And emerald light.
The Innkeeper came down the stairs
                    One flight.
"Could have been one of you
                    Who lies upstairs
Half dead...
But drink to your Life...
Yes!
                    Pour down your lies.
Murmur in the corners.
                    It's no surprise!"
He returned to his well-worn station
                    After collecting his evening's tabs
There he watched all of their faces
                    All of the desperate and all of the sad...
Just about midnight
                    The full moon shone

Through the doorway
        Window.

                Like a ghost on a rose.

The clock on the wall
                    Spoke in chimes of early morning hours
Displaying its array of carven animals...
A dancing Unicorn frozen in the frieze
                    Brawling bears captured...woven into trees
Where weathered looks of lonely stags
                    Watched with wooden stares
Over the sea
            Of faces.
Every man silent now
As they trickled
                    Into the streets...
Made their way
                    To the place
Where they might lie down
Till the Dawn put on her
                    Dressing gown.
The countryside was sleeping
Lustrous was
                    The night...
A galloping of horses
Was the only sound...
                    The only sound...
Three horsemen were riding...
                    Riding god-speed into town...

One man was handsome.
An ivory-handled pistol at
His
Hand.
The second man a vagrant
Stubbly face beneath the
Cocked
Hat on his brow.
The third man was wealthy
With an air
Of elegant
Grace.
All looking over the highways
Looking through all the byways
For the Innkeeper's place.
They looked
But could not find it...
They rode over sleeping indigo fields
Till the watchtowers chimed at three...

At every door they went
                    A-knocking…
As a cold mist blew off the moor…
In the full moonlight
They looked like the reapers
                    Of earth's abandoned souls…
A cold wind was a-blowing
As they rode about the town
The first one stopped…dismounted
Then fed his steed some hay.
The other two looked down
Then said,
                    "Shouldn't we wait till
                              The light of day?"
No one spoke to the naked darkness
                    Then two more found their feet
Upon the frozen street.
They walked so…so slowly
                    Ever so slowly
Their darkened eyes set in their heads.
Not a word they spoke…
They walked,
          Oh, so slowly
Like
     The
          Reapers
               Of
                    The
                         Dead…
They walked,
          Oh, so slowly
Up to the Innkeeper's door.
Where inside the Innkeeper was a-washing
                    The swill, the dirt, the grime…
Preparing to make his chores a shorter task
                    So to take his leave for sleeping.

"The night so long…
        So long
                This night
Just want to make my bed."
When at the door came a-knocking
A-knocking at his door.
His breath almost strangled breathless
As he made his way across the floor.
The Unicorn stood watching
From the statuesque
                Carven clock…
The chimes sang like a cathedral choir
        At this morn's hour of four o'clock.

The heavy wooden door
                    Creaked slowly
The darkness merged with
                    The candlelight inside…
Three men spoke and then asked,
                    "Could we please come inside?"
"The night is cold
                    The wind so fast
Too hard
        Too long
                To ride…"
The Innkeeper stayed hesitant and wary
As he led the three inside…
The rich
        The vagrant
                    The handsome
To his table they did stride.
"State your business,"
                    The Innkeeper implored.
The wind outside was howling
It shuddered at the door.

The handsome man was fumbling
                    With something
Inside
        His
                Coat.
The man with the stubbly beard
With a hand
                His face
                        Did smote.
The wealthy man leaned back
As he's the one who spoke.
"There's a man we're looking for
S'been said
                    He's come this way...
Been like a ghost
            To
                    All
                            Of us.
S'never been seen in the light of day.
Been riding over
        Foothills
                And coves... far and below.
Not seen his face before...
Please tell us
        If
                You
                        Can,
                            The way he came to go."
The handsome man was twitching
Then said,
                    "This man's a witch!
He's agile with his mind
                    And when he came for me one night

Was so inclined
        To steal
            My
                Soul
                    From
                        Me.
So I've come to
        See
            Him
                Die…
Only then will my soul
            Be mine."
"That's so."
            The wretched man spoke,
"He's keen with sword
            And knife.
I know it well
And a
        Bell
            Rings
                In
                    Hell.
And I know what name it calls."
        In unison they rose.
The Innkeeper said,
                "I'm closed.
But a bed might be made
            For you
                This cruel night."
"Thank you."
            They said,
'We're all so close to dead
That our sleep might be
            Done
                This night."
"Stay here then,"

The Innkeeper said.

While there arose

Inside the Innkeeper's head

A voice…it seemed

Coming from

The dead.

"Climb these stairs to where I live…

Come upstairs

To where I lie."

Someone was going to die!

The Innkeeper went

Up the stairs one flight

Expecting the man he found at his door

Half-dead…

Already dead by this night…

The door

Was invitingly

Opened

As if by the howling wind…

A solitary man

Sat calmly inside…

Resting still…

Sitting beside the bed.

No windows

Were thrust

Open.

So how was this to be?

The

Solitary

Man

Had not one life…

But three!

He was wealthy

From his clothing…

And handsome

Was his face…

A stubbly beard had grown there,
As he stood with
                                An elegant grace.
An ivory pistol hung
                                Near his waistcoat
As he turned to the Innkeeper
                                Then said,
"'Tis 'bout time I ride
                                For three souls
Will search for me.
                        When I'm found
                                The news will be, I'm dead."
Said the Innkeeper,
                        "There are three men
                                who wait downstairs
                                                For you."
The Solitary Man slowly smiled…
The new morning light was seething
                        Like a fire
                                Burning inside the curtain lace…
With early crimson light
                        Before the sun is bold and bright.
"They've gone for now,"
                        Said the Solitary Man with his secret smile.
"I must move with a swift and steady pace,
                        For tonight
Three horsemen will be following
                        And I must
Stay ahead
                        Till light."
Then the two men walked down the hallway
And
        Down
                The
                        Stairs
                                One flight.

There was no one in the barroom
No one was

                              Since that night.

Three horses stood

                    In waiting…

                                        Waiting by the door.

The solitary man took all three…

                    Then looked the Innkeeper in the eye and said,
"I'll take the horses with me.

                    Tonight they'll use their feet."

And off he rode

                    To the end of town

With a sob heard,

          Then

                    A shriek.

The solitary man
                    Went riding…riding…
Riding with the utmost speed…
Every night the Innkeeper keeps vigil
For a man, half-dead
                    In the street,
With three souls
                    Ardently following
Walking slowly
        On their
                Feet.
Tonight there'll be a full moon
When the mist's swept
                    Off
                            The moor.
Could tonight there be a knocking?
A knocking
            On
                The
                        Innkeeper's
                            Door?

The Innkeeper

This poem is actually a story based on an old poem entitled "The Highwayman." I wrote this poem one night after thinking about the elements of the old poem. "The Highwayman" ends in tragedy as the highwayman dies while trying to escape the authorities. The innkeeper's daughter who waits for him, not knowing he has been killed, continually looks out her window, wondering what happened to her lover. The innkeeper was one of those uncharismatic characters that I thought would be interesting to develop, but with a story endowed with its own haunted history.

This is a very long poem with seven drawings, each of them unique to the telling of the story. The first illustration is the "Medieval Barroom." I had to do this drawing in sections as the telling of the story/poem has a setting where the innkeeper keeps order in the house. I needed a stairway, a room for the patrons, and an entryway isolated from both. At the doorway is a shadow of a man standing, which begins the long sad tale.

The second illustration is called "Ghost on a Rose." The intention here is to create some foreshadowing of what comes later in the poem. I used a white rose bathing in the moonlight to give this effect.

The third illustration is named "Three Riders." Looking closely, you can see the three horsemen riding toward a stone bridge leading into a populated area as they attempt to find the innkeeper's place.

The fourth illustration is "The Clock." Here the description given earlier in the poem takes form. Notice the time on the clock as the poem progresses.

The fifth illustration is "The Innkeeper." The innkeeper has just opened the door to see who knocked. I wanted him to look very wary as he peers out behind the half-opened door.

The sixth illustration called "Three Horses" comes well after a lengthy dialogue with all the characters that has funneled into this moment. The illustration shows three horses tied up just outside the inn in the coming sunrise. It is a pivotal moment in the poem, and I felt the details needed to be put into form.

The last illustration is called 'Sunrise/Sunset" and is particularly important as it is the final explanation of the coexisting entities. Only one can exist in the daylight hours, and the other three can only exist in the darkness. I used the sun on the top of the drawing to symbolize sunrise and split it on the underside for one half of the full moon. In the sunrise is the solitary man taking the three horses, and in the moonlight, the other three struggle through the brush, trying to catch up.

Sandcastles

Sandcastles

We live in a world of children
Building simple castles made of sand
Things we build always rise and fall
Beneath envied laughs and jeers…
Kicks and shoves…
Of children fighting children
Destroying every dream
Crushing towered aspirations
Within a wash of tears…
As if castles will not fall
By Time's decay
In winds and rain…
As ancient ledgers
Held in weathered fingers
Turn those tallowed sheets
Where pride's destiny
Hid virtue between forgotten pages
Read silently into the flow of tides…
We came to walk the far horizons
Reaching these sandy shores to dream
Leaving our unnoticed footprints imprinted
On the places where we've been
These sands of life rearranged by time
As the sea moves beyond our sight
Washing these worn footpaths away…
Places we walked together through
While holding hands with suffered sight
In the dark we wove a dream of light
Hoping…beyond winds and tears
Kicks and shoves…

Laughs and jeers…
Never stopping,
Allowing virtue to fall from
Our pockets
Or drive our hands
Into the furious sands of fools…
And when we have gone
When no traces stand
To mark us
What man might show his wisdom
Of things that were or might have been?
For the sandcastles he finds searching
Are just mounds of sand that's fallen
Beneath the faultless, timeless rushes
Of the sea…

Sandcastles

andcastles! It seemed like such an easy cliché! Just draw a few sensational sandcastles and all done…but I just couldn't go there! While the quick and easy solution seemed a good way to go this time, the poem really steered me away from the obvious.

To avoid the potential rut of merely drawing a sandcastle, I had to again study a lot of material! Architecture, landscape, stones, and walls were all areas I considered! I found drawing a lot of sand seemed uninteresting….even with a cool sandcastle! Eventually, I came up with the right mix of color and design, yet still analytical of the composition, that it would be an interpretation of the poem! Not always an easy process!

The poem "Sandcastles" is a cautionary work that tells us to avoid the pitfalls of judging differences and, perhaps, eccentricities of our fellow travelers as we go about living our time here. In the end, we are merely sandcastles that will eventually erode within the mechanisms of time. Even the physical things we built to last will eventually blow away in the final moments within the dust…long after we've placed our last footsteps. Do not allow "pride's destiny" to hide "virtue within the hidden pages." Build lives based on compassion for each other. In the end, it will be all that really matters!

The Poetry of Wind

The Poetry of Wind

The poetry of wind…
Is not of wounded words
Or chains of brandished
Sentences placed
In incongruent display
Like rails of steel
Frozen in bitter soil…

Nor does it sigh
In a melancholy melody
Like songbirds'
Or nightingales'
Flailing notes
Unwritten against all
Man's darkness…

The poetry of wind…
Is the story of all
It sees and has seen
Over all of time
Always finding two
Hearts together
Like yours and mine…

The Poetry of Wind

This is the illustration for the poem named "The Poetry of Wind." This one is a variation of ink, ink washes, dry and oil pastels, and charcoal! Did a number of sketches before I decided on the actual work! I overexaggerated the woman's hair and skirt to show the effects of wind blowing over the couple. The brown-colored bird is my representation of the nightingale mentioned in the poem. The ruined rail tracks represent our human failures, or perhaps our deteriorating footprint on the lands we once believed were under our control, now consumed in nature's reclamation.

The poem has a mystical romanticism incorporating some uncommon concepts. Man-made elements decaying within time's insidious course fall beneath the wind's grasp of the burgeoning beauty of nature surrounding it. Yet even as the wind follows its path over humanity, it also sees beauty in the nature of our compassion for each other. So the wind has become the witness, in its elemental form, which neither judges nor condemns! It merely sees and then moves on, carrying memories.

The Desert of the Lost

The Desert of the Lost

As I lay under a spreading oak
      And the wind swept across my brow
My mind fell prey to a gentle breeze
      And was carried for many miles
Caressed in its many dreams of peace
      I found myself at ease
Then it laid me in the crags and rocks
      And dashed across the sea
It left me in a barren place
      A place I've never seen
And I found in myself an emptiness
      Left by the gentle breeze

The Desert of the Lost

"The Desert of the Lost" was created using several ink washes, acrylics, luminescent inks, and dry pastels. Though the title seems to lend itself to a more arid location, the meaning of the poem diverges from the obvious. Deserts can often be places of isolation, which, for this poem, was the situation. I had to create a place of isolation yet incorporate the concept of a "spreading oak" throughout. So with this intention, I placed a figure of a young man stranded on the barren stones of a bleak mountain range nestled in fog. There is no refuge, no place he can continue with any secure footing, so he must remain here, wondering how he will survive. Like looking through an oval frame, I wanted the oak tree to be an extension of the stones from where the figure was seated. As you see, the oak tree follows the lines of the stones and sprouts from it. Into the trunk I drew miniature trees, finally ending the loop with draping flowers.

This is the illustration I created for this poem! It is certainly not the best thing I ever wrote, but it certainly was the most important!

At fourteen years old, I had a writing assignment to do for English class. I was to create a short story of my own! I thought I did a pretty fair job of it, but it needed something else, so I wrote and incorporated this poem. I took the story to my father and asked what he thought. When he was finished reading, he asked where I had found the poem since it fit in well with the story. When I told him I wrote it, he was very impressed and told me, "I can see you have a soul that speaks to you! You should write more. Write things that matter… If you write anything at all, make it worth reading."

I never forgot, and I never stopped writing after that.

My first poem!

Grapevines

Grapevines

When the berries grew
Just outside the windowpane
They were so near
And never missed
Did you think
To the day ahead
When the vines would fail
Like roots taken to the deep forest
Then be missed?
When your days are long
Yearning to remember
The taste of nature's wine
Sweet the scents
Once near at hand
Gone one day
To flourish in a distant land
Remember then while you journey
Looking for the meaning of Life
To pause just outside your window
To count the grapevines
That in your vineyard lie

Grapevines

"Grapevines" is a poem that tries to infer we should appreciate the things we have near us while they are here. This would include not only material things, but also people who are precious to us.

Trying to come up with an artistic concept for the poem "Grapevines" was a difficult venture. Getting the right composition of elements seemed to be the biggest challenge. The poem is a very short one with a very conventional theme. Though it seemed it was going to be an easy project, trying to create an illustration that would be meaningful became a challenge. The concept of a figure near a grapevine seemed a likely concept. Yet the right combination of elements was essential to create this in some artistic but believable way. Most vineyards trellis their vines so they are easily picked. This, though beautiful in its own way, was very uninteresting as a drawing. Also the poem leaned more to wildly growing vines that looked productive, though haphazardly growing over something more interesting than a trellis.

I created the drawing using a half-nude female model to display the comforting nonchalance of casual acceptance of the remote surroundings where the warm environment makes the grapes prolific. The irony exists in the aperture created in a stone archway where the impending cold swept off the distant mountains will ultimately end the life of the grapevines and force the woman toward a more compatible environment where she can survive.

The drawing has blends of charcoal pencils, graphic pencils, pastels, oil pastels, and luminescent inks. Eventually the blends meshed together after nearly two months of preparation.

Leaves

Leaves

I saw the leaves
Falling to the forest's floor
In the fading light of crimson gold
Watched their failed tenacity
Become a final prayer...
Evolving to remembrance where
Days were dreams of kinder times
Begotten over silver water wistfully
Spilling over timeless green places
Giving hope...that gentle virtue...a time to stay...
Inside the songs of autumn wind
Resound hollow voices echoing refrains
It kept them alive
When the summer died
Closing them inside the departing light
Chained mercilessly to its melancholy melody...
I thought I heard them cry
A long and tender sigh...
In such a solemn quiet hush...
So meandering and still...
Then watched them falling
Upon the rested ground
Without a cry, a whimper, or a sound...

Leaves

The poem "Leaves" is about the grace of dying. The thought came to me one fall day as I watched the leaves quietly falling from a large maple tree. It came to me the world is made of a complex array of seasons where everything in it has a period of time to flourish and then depart as the world moves on. It was the graceful descent of the leaves that made me feel how we should approach the time in our lives when we too shall depart.

The technical difficulty with this piece has been the most complex array of mediums I've attempted! The underlying drawing took about a month to complete, and then the task of putting colors to it without losing the integrity of the drawing was complicated! So overall, there are several ink washes over most of the immediate foreground, followed with dry pastels, oil pastels, pastel pencil, charcoal pencils, charcoal, ink pen, and some acrylic paint! Yet to be honest, the drawing doesn't feel complete to me. I continued to look at it for almost a week, as you now see it, and could not figure it out! So I decided to let it stand as it is!

The poem has a dark side that is well portrayed by the illustration. The meanings, both as a poem and as artwork, I leave for your interpretation.

Untitled #4

Untitled # 4

When I realized there were more years behind me than there were before, I knew the chance to join that great symphony of life was slipping away. To live a span of twenty years might be a lifetime, but even ten, five, or one could be a lifetime of beauty and discovery if the right person is there to share it. I do not know what fate bestows upon my corporeal soul, but in the infinite, I know those sweet memories will not depart.

I write against the dying light, and still, I am in wonder of hope. My lines, barely discerned by feeble eyes and an unsteady hand, grope with the threads of destiny whispering reverberations over the tides of advancing shadows. While darkness folds itself into the last remains of this crimson field of sky, I watch a glimmer, like a star that lost its way into the heavens, write its epitaph upon the final skylight...

We are points of mortal light
Neither twixt nor twain
And if we lived in a starry night
Our light would be a flame
To coax the moon from its flight
Across the harbored moors
Our light would beacon all above
In Life...In Love...Adored...

Untitled #4

I completed this drawing for some casual writing I eventually called "Untitled #4." It's an unorthodox change from the traditional poetry I usually write; however, I felt it was important to keep it as originally written. There was a lot to work with visually, so I simply incorporated some of the main themes into it.

In the drawing, I wanted a writing desk beside a window. The window needed to be the portal for the scarlet sky as it designed the pretense of nightfall. Some of my original ventures proved either too complex or too simplified. After reexamining the meanings contained in "Untitled #4," I felt the window, wall, and desk also needed some human hands writing words on scattered pages. Drawing everything as I imagined, entranced by a window (even a large one), did not fulfill the intentions of the writings. When I considered the fundamentals I'd chosen to create the drawing, I realized the true meanings of the writings existed beyond the confines I considered. The "star that lost its way to the heavens" was an essential aspect that needed to be incorporated.

I had to consider how to integrate a star and maintain the integrity of my original perception of the drawing. To create starlight in its own atmosphere, I had to bring the interior setting to the outside or bring the outside setting to the interior room (which I originally hoped to do as a window). Often when I am caught in this kind of paradox, I find my creative side lurking just below the conscious level, so I went to work on a solution. What I needed, as the writings clearly suggested, was a kind of illusion where both realities existed. When I came to this theory, I worked the solid elements (window, wall, desk, and hands writing on papers) into the drawing and simply faded them to nonexistence when their perspective became unessential. The scarlet-orange skies were formed over a barren rocky landscape, and I finalized the drawing with two stars in the sky (as one star would find the other).

The materials used were fairly standard: dry pastels, oil pastels, and a small amount of inking. The theme is one of reminiscence, discovery, and a sense of longing we all feel in our lives.

Untitled #5

Untitled #5

Like veils blown apart
By an unwelcome wind
Sleep departs...
Opening those harsh doors
Into the Land of Waking.
With deliberate steps...
Whispering...fading
Into echoes gone silent...
Sleep crawls away...
Emerging alone as a wounded warrior
Into the native day...
Searching again for elusive peace
Only he can find...
Within words written
Inside shadowy dark pages
There exhausting the hours
Of tumult and chaos
Discovers tranquil words
Among confusions and toils
Counting too little Peace
Into his gathering of spoils
Struggling through every one
With each fading light
To bring them home again...
When the Day is Night...

Untitled #5

The theme is a little whimsical and really originates from twenty-two years working as an RN on nights. The concept was to personify "sleep" as an entity resembling a wounded soldier. I came up with the concept after spending another frustrating sleep-deprived night, thinking how elusive sleep seemed to be. The idea of a soldier, crippled and wounded by the ravages of day-to-day life, seemed an appropriate metaphor. As he wandered off into the morning light, he would look for peace and bring it home as each night began, hoping to comfort the sleeper with peaceful dreams. Not always easy, the soldier rarely finds enough solace to ensure total peace. The dreams are hard, keeping us restless...

The drawing was quite an undertaking. The concept was difficult, and the underlying drawing took almost two weeks to create. To establish the context, an ink wash was placed over most of the drawing and then highlighted with pastels. Afterward, I did not like the effect this created, so I redrew some of the landmarks to simplify the drawing. Eventually, the basis of what I originally intended started to emerge. Still, the concept of light was not something I could create with black-and-white shades without diminishing the content of the drawing. This created a need to form light with colors to produce the effects I wanted.

Eventually I used both oil pastels and dry pastels to establish landmarks to show light filtering through the doorway. Some finishing touches were done using drawing pens and touches of acrylic paint. As I said, it was quite an undertaking.

Untitled #22

Untitled #22

Sleeping disregarded words
Lie here remembering chanted chords
Played melodies engraved on metal gears
Where fluttering chime's memories lost
Their hollow dances inside the broken clock...
Here my eclectic epiphany remains
Mixed with the crustaceous halves
Of time, remembering the place
Where the middle has forgotten
Its beginnings and its end...

Words awakened realized
There was more magic in your eyes
Than watching a lifetime of starlight falling...
Where solace and peace
Stared wordlessly beneath a wondrous sky
Captured inside infinite boundaries...
In these words I dared to dream...
In these words I sought deliverance...
In this heart I found my love...
These words are the compass of my soul
Where true directions are not defined
But found in fragile lands of our abandon
Where serendipity plays in summer fields
Erudite of the tangled pains of winter's passing...

The hidden light's revelation
Spilled glowing baskets of yarn and thread
Scattered skeins sweetly patterned
In disarrayed colors
Carelessly tossed into the burgeoning sky…
Unbridled hands
Wove them softly
Into quiet grasses
Sleeping beneath verdant waves
Of a zephyr's breath
As it searches green meadows
Where the languid catnip summer
Curls itself into quiet dreams…

There Time sits unseen
In a darkened chair
Weaving designs intricate with words
Beautifully written like forgotten songs
A lost harmony of symphonic notes
Bleeding with intersecting threads
Lovingly sewn into cloth-spun light…
We lie inside this woven blanket
Evolving hope in our whisperings
With longings caressed in valorous grace
Those passions eternally written
On the forgotten pages where
The hand of time marks the voyage
Where our hearts will ever roam…

Untitled #22

The theme of this poem is multileveled as it begs the questions, what is time, and does it really matter as we enter relationships and then, sometimes without our knowledge or interventions, move on to other situations? However, there are those times when everything aligns, and we actually find someone who inspires us to be more than what we thought we could ever be. There is always someone you never want to let go.

Here my eclectic epiphany remains
Mixed with the crustaceous halves
Of time remembering the place
Where the middle has forgotten
Its beginnings and its end…

In these words I dared to dream…
In these words I sought deliverance…
In this heart I found my love…
These words are the compass of my soul
Where true directions are not defined

This is the illustration for "Untitled #22." There was a lot of imagery to work with, so I took my time incorporating most of it into the drawing. The complexity of undertaking this one made me utilize a number of mediums. First was the underlying pencil drawing, several ink washes, acrylic paints, dry and oil pastels, charcoal, luminous inks, and finally, ink highlights! I feel like I redid every line on the drawing a hundred times! However, I do feel I did the poem justice with the illustration!

In All My Dreams Lost

In All My Dreams Lost

Did you ever Dream?
In the morning's discerning light
Did the dream
Grow inside your conscious self
To be born?
Or banished?
Imprisoned inside you
In some dark place
Never to be seen again?
You still feel it
Aching against a heart
That keeps on beating
Wounding every second…
Pounding…
Hammering…
Thrashing…
Defeating…
Until it dies
In a small oblivion unseen…
Silent…
Concealed …
Unspoken…
Gone…
I am full of flaws…
These are a map of my wounds
With no names…
They were my dreams once…
Now…they are my scars…

In All My Dreams Lost

"In All My Dreams Lost" is about feeling regret surrounding opportunities we hoped to seize or, perhaps foolishly, thought we would accomplish. Either real or imagined, the losses everyone experiences places cruel shards of grief and regret into our hearts. It wounds us, then it heals…with a scar.

Creating the illustration for "In All My Dreams Lost" took a lot of introspection. I needed a human figure without status symbols (clothes, signs of obvious wealth, jewelry, and so forth) to represent the innocent aspect of human nature. That illustration could be either sitting or lying beside/near a reflective surface. In this reflection would be a side portrayed in the coarse brutal reality he/she existed in with a reflection beyond it revealing every "opportunity/aspiration/fortune/love" hoped for…out of reach, never to be seized.

My first choice of reflective objects was obviously a mirror. Eventually, I started several sketches on how this would work out on the final copy and realized my choice of a mirror was not workable. When considering all earthly materials with reflective surfaces, I thought a pool of reflecting water might work better than the reflection from a mirror. So my second round of multiple sketches took place with better results. The elements I chose in both the upper and lower parts of the illustration are indicative of a harsh ugly reality above the waterline, as opposed with the pleasant unrealized dreams beneath the surface.

Untitled #7

Untitled #7

Before I draw that veil
Of sleep before my eyes...
Before those dreams
Held by tender arms enclose...
Before my whispered words
Fall into night's repose
Let me usher perfumes
Of scented prose
And crystalline lines
Of sentences into
Places where your soul is sleeping...
And I shall awaken there
Before the amber light of day
Places its first step upon the ground...
I stand here in this tender field
Unfurled flag that found its country...
A hand discovered...
A place where twin hearts
Beat as one...

Untitled #7

"Untitled #7" is a love poem. The central theme revolves around "an unfurled flag that found its country," which is what I based the illustration upon. The female figure sitting beneath the tree in a somewhat dreamlike state and the flag behind her are made of the same two colors, showing the connection between them.

The drawing was created using a basic pencil sketch rendered with dry pastels for the basic backgrounds. I used oil pastels for most of the foreground, including the female figure. To bring up some of the colors in the background, acrylic paints assisted me to distinguish flowers and vegetation.

Windsongs

Windsongs

"**W**indsongs" is about losing yourself in the wild core of nature, discovering you must belong there, having returned after a long absence. Using the wind as a construct to see wilderness in its most elemental form is a fantasy neither I nor anyone will ever see. Still the idea of it sits inside my thoughts, and its ponderance gives me peace.

Though it is not an abstract concept, the development of this drawing was so intense, I actually abandoned it for several months and went on to another project. My problems with this particular drawing stemmed from a lack of finding any natural subjects to draw from. I could not direct my creativity toward the drawing in such a way to make it even marginally believable. I did a few other projects and then came back a few months later. Eventually, with a few untried mediums (acrylics and inking), I was able to get the effects I wanted to the degree I felt it was completed.

Looking at the Sun

Looking at the Sun

There are places
Captured within the heart and soul
That crave those melodies
The leaves sing to the sunlight
In a cloudless sky…

And all those things of worth…
Become neither worthy,
Nor visible…
To us…or to we…
Standing, invincible,
Believing in something
Inconsequential…

Petals of sunlight
Fall over the earth
Showing us where we see
The glories lying beyond us…
What we believe in understanding
Washes away the blindness
To look into infinity…

Looking at the Sun

"Looking at the Sun" is dedicated to a concept where the revelations visible within the beauty of sunlight expose the intensity of life as it is presented to us each and every day. We all have our troubles, but when they are unraveled against the infinite timeline, they are barely noticed…hardly worth mentioning! As the poem suggests, "And all those things of worth… Become neither worthy, nor visible…To us…or to we…"

The creation of this illustration was easier than most. I needed an expansive setting with sunlight in full measure. Adding a tree into the mixture placed one of the elements of the poem into the overall concept.

The illustration was created with an underlying pencil drawing, which was later colored by dry pastels, and a tree was added using acrylics. Overall, it worked out better than I thought it would.

Fog Tigers

Fog Tigers

Borne innocent to our noble youth
Till time scoured sins in our bones
There was a time before the hour of early waking
Before the gray mists of morning rose
My days would take on their thunder
While the night dust of sleep then froze
The darkness of dreams to my unconscious sight
Where Fog Tigers leapt at my windowless night
Scowling with sharp phantom claws
Fear poured itself into glasses
And one by one, I drank them down
There Snow Dragons rose all about me
Captured by the full light of the moon
Fear pounded deep into my soul inside
While I tried to release my primal animal cry
And lose whatever I thought to be my Truth
When at last the gray morning mist surrounded me
My eyes beseeched the sun
Washing all the veiled blindness from around me
Until the Fog Tigers and Snow Dragons
Were undone…

Fog Tigers

This poem is about nightmares or night terrors as some may call them. Many times as I tried to fall to sleep, especially after working nights, my mind refused to settle. I wrote this one afternoon when I should have been sleeping after pulling my third twelve-hour shift in a row.

"Fog Tigers" had lot of material to work with visually, and I tried to include most of it into the illustration. The female figure, placed in the midst of this melee, was drawn partially covered. It was drawn with the intention of assigning vulnerability to a sleeper being tormented by aggressors that may or may not truly be there. Nonetheless, the sleep is tortured, coupled with a suffered disquiet. The inherent peace we expect, when we close our eyes for sleep, is forever robbed by fog tigers and snow dragons of our own conscious or unconscious making.

Coming up with the details for this one was difficult not only for models but also the execution of a nightmare scene. The tigers were fairly easy to find, but two dragons that would fit into the picture were not easy to locate. After looking at hundreds of dragons, I found parts of a dozen I could manage and come up with something workable. The tigers, though prolific, never seemed to have the stance I wanted for the illustration. Again I used several sketches of tigers before I tried them on the larger work. I wanted tangled dark ruins behind the sleeper to further the concept of a nightmare. This endeavor was very tedious, but the effect was what I hoped for. The complexity makes it an interesting piece.

Untitled #10

Untitled # 10

The early hours of morning
Are snow-covered fields
Overspread with memories of summer grass
Their naked yellow arms
Thrust unyieldingly
Steadfast with hope
Above the snow-salted ground…
When night realized
The Land discovered
Those cold wounds of winter
Cut into mortal stone
It froze the world in darkness…
Printed on pages icy and thin
Hieroglyphs inscribed with unwavering mortality
Remain unread by the lost desires of Men…

Legends told me an obscure story…
"There are magical powers
In the first snow…"
But by who
And for whom
I have never known…

Windsongs

I have gone
Closer to the wind
Listening to the stories
It tells…
Where it walked against
Wild green palaces
And washed the eaves
Of angel's tongues…
It spoke in words
I could not hear
Like lost songs
Only the heart
Holds dear…

Its very nature is a gown
Delicately white
Like poetry conceived
Within the ear of the world...
A soft whisper spoken
To the pallid sunrise...
A song carried by the wind
Soughing itself into naked branches
Worshipping the sky...
Her legend forever carried
In mouths of ravens, swans,
And unicorns...
Existing together in this mythos
Of an enduring romance
Without borders...
Without ending...

And still the whitened sepulchre lingers...
A wavering witness and wayfaring wanderer
Searching Winter's inspired domains...
Fear of its icy grasp does not
Conquer my heart
My soul burns with a feral flame
Each thought of you a burning ember
Each kiss is an all-consuming fire
Within your embrace
The blanket of snow disappears
Revealing the naked beauty
Hidden beneath
Winter's whitened cloak

Untitled #10

"Untitled #10" is a poem about finding love over the last of our earthly seasons. It sees the beauty of winter's start but, by the end of the poem, realizes compassion still lives behind, a sometimes cloaked, sometimes cold, or perhaps exists inside an impassive exterior.

> Fear of its icy grasp does not
> Conquer my heart
> My soul burns with a feral flame
> Each thought of you a burning ember

The illustration was fairly complex! I wanted the cruelty of winter's domain to be prevalent over the entire drawing while trying to carve a haven of refuge into it. The suggestion of the imminent dominion of winter existing on the next mountainside while portraying a closer threshold's impending reality of snow needed to be integrated. This included placing a silhouette of a couple somewhere in the landscape. So again, I began the search for possible landscape pictures where I could get ideas. Eventually, I utilized around a dozen landscape pictures and over a half dozen pictures of couples and then started to draw. The result of working every concept I found into what I envisioned created what became the illustration I called "Untitled # 10."

Untitled #24

Untitled #24

Do not let me live too fast…
To breathe
To breathe the air
That succulent breath
The one I remember
The one I remember so well
As if time wove into itself
Colored sweet air
With joy…and breath…
And life…
As it were one day…
A day I would never
Want to pass
A breath
I would take again
And again…
Breathing its memory in
So I would never forget…
Do not let me live
Too fast…

Untitled #24

The poem "Untitled #24" is a short poem that says to enjoy "life" in the moment. Times like these may never come again. These are the treasures we gather as pleasant memories we plant in our hearts. Too often we live our lives so quickly, we find no joy in the paths we have chosen. Many of us overlook or miss the opportunities to find any solace or satisfaction in the journey. We search our lives trying to find what gives us peace when it was always right in front of us.

The drawing depicts a couple enjoying the day among a flower-filled field with ancient ruins close by. I chose this depiction to show the ancient remains falling apart as nature continues to flourish in spite of everything deteriorating. The couple will grow old, the ruins will disintegrate into rubble over time, and the world the couple knew will disappear. Yet that day will remain in their memory for as long as they exist.

A day I would never
Want to pass
A breath
I would take again
And again…
Breathing its memory in
So I would never forget…

Untitled #12

Untitled #12

Still…
The taste of your kiss
Lingers…
Still…
Your touch
Maps lines on the skin of my back…
Still…
The air of your breath
Is caught in my hair…
Still…
Your eyes
Are the memory I see…
Still…
To feel the depth of your heart's
Surrender…
Is to know
You have captured mine…

Untitled #12

"Untitled #12" is a romanticized writing about feelings we sometimes cannot put into words. I considered renaming the poem "Still," but felt the poem needed to retain some of its enigma and remains as one of my untitled poems.

This is the first time I attempted watercolors in a drawing. Behind the silhouetted figures in the foreground, I used watercolors to put in the sky. Otherwise, the drawing is a combination of inking, pastels, and a dabbling of acrylics. The effect is rather simple, but I felt the overall attempt worked out very well.

Touching Forever

Touching Forever

Into a place I never met
Flowers blow in
Rippled waves
Sewn by a weaving wind
Crafting their works
Beneath the lonely sight
Of pearl white clouds…
Touching forever
In a horizon so near and so far
I could not tell the difference
As to where the sky began
And the earth ended…

Timeless voices beckoned …
Their echoes of ruined thunder
Mocked the places
Where raindrop's failing whispers
Tapped their final silence
Upon the ancient stones…
Crushed innocence released itself
Into those fallen dreams
Lost inside the many pools of tears
Forsaken beneath fading
Clouds of surrender…

Across these lonely lands
Alone she stands
Her distant cross
A monument

Impaled upon mountain's rock
Feeling too mortal...incomplete...
Emblazoned with a grievous scar
From many battles unprepared to fight
Imprisoned within this place abandoned
Lost in Time's irreverent discourse...

Bestowed upon humanity's hopeful few...
Are those whose understanding
Could only persist imperfectly
Scarcely clothed with naked prayers
Exhausted with earthen Science and its lost Magic
They confess their undetermined losses
Like scattered pottery
Lying broken like genuflections
Ruined over crumbling rocks...
They're bowing heads with sobering humility
As they simply wait and watch...

He journeyed there beside her
To find the secret life beneath all things...
Inside fleeting moments of fire
The pilgrim Journey felt immortal...
His undecided steps
Never contained the wanderings
Through the many failed glimmerings
Where their frozen shadows
Washed over
The endless spent wax monuments
Where once they believed
Forever contained them...
Only in the courageous light
Held against the darkening sky
Will discovery of a secret unfurl...

Compassionate Warrior
Who watches and waits
Without a weapon wielded
Replaced the warrior's blade
With a courageous heart raised
Against the burgeoning darkness
Like an exhausted broken sword
Beseeching the sun...
Within his broken words
These offered prayers he seized
Humbly begging it to yield
As he asked the passing sky
To hold its place forever...

Wisdom tells many things
Start and end with hope...
His offered heart raised
To the passing sky
Her loss he offers to complete
The sky inspired by his reverence
Held a moment out of time
To relent...
To gaze upon them
In a perpetual glance
And stilled them inside
A timeless embrace

In a place some may never meet
Together they stand
Within rippled waves of a weaving wind
Beneath lonely pearl white clouds
Touching forever
In a horizon so near and so far
You cannot tell the difference...
Where the earth ends...
And the sky begins...

Touching Forever

"*T*ouching Forever" is a poem about losing someone to breast cancer. It carves a reality so close to my heart, it fills my blood with promises…and those are promises I must keep.

As a registered nurse of forty-two years, I encountered too many people whose lives were irrevocably altered/changed by the words *breast cancer*. I use the term *people* instead of the term *women* because the effects of breast cancer goes far beyond the women (and sometimes men) diagnosed with this disease. Watching your mother, grandmother, spouse, daughter, sister, aunt, or friend go through this experience is heartrending. Most of us are forced (by the nature of the disease) to sit on the sidelines as observers or witnesses with no real capacity to carry any of the burden for them. It weighs heavily on every family member, every close friend, and everyone who wants to help. However, in this finite world, the breast cancer patient truly carries the burden alone. This truth weighs heavily on me, remembering how my late wife finally succumbed to her countless battles, fighting it with the last of her strength for over eighteen years. She died in 2011.

Before she died, in innumerable conversations with her, she asked me to "not let her be forgotten." It is a promise I took to heart, and it is a promise I have honored. Rather than elaborate on everything she did to help breast cancer patients over her eighteen years of survival, I will tell you to look into two books I wrote about her. The first one is *Seasons in Cancer*, and the other one is named *Sunset under the Poet's Tree*. And that is all I will say about them, save one item.

The initial inspiration behind the illustration for this poem is located within the pages of *Season in Cancer* and is named "Completion."

"Touching Forever" was written for every person whose lives have been affected by breast cancer. The poem was created integrating more fable into it than fact. It is a kind of story-poem that I hope will shine some understanding light on some very dark, almost insurmountable challenges. By the poem's end, the hardships they faced together become the monument by which they are remembered.

The illustration for "Touching Forever" was extremely difficult to create. After months of research and innumerable sketches, I felt I created some semblance of what I envisioned. The drawing is a mixture of pastels, oil pastels, ink washes, acrylics, and some inking as well. Notice the foreground. There you find numerous scattered objects and symbols that have meaning and exist as elements in the poem.

I'm a Country Road

I'm a Country Road

Just a ribbon of green
Lyin' against the trees
And you can run for a while
For a stretch of miles
Breathing in the sweet air
Just like you know
It's the way… it always should be…

       Well, I'm a country road…
       Can't you hear me singing
       A country road…
       Can't you feel me winging
       A country road…
       Don't you want to dream
       Like you wanted to dream?

In the autumn air
My leaves colored wine
With the smell of vines
And the rocks and trees
They're a part of me
That can set you free
In a world made of leaves…

       Well, I'm a country road…
       Can't you smell the air here?
       A country road…
       Can't you feel the life here?
       A country road…
       Don't you want to see
       What it's like to be free?

In the winter's spree
Blowin' through the trees
And the air's frozen gown
Stirs the snow on the ground
Hanging thin icy whirls
Like cathedral spires…
That it hangs in the trees…

Well, I'm a country road…
Where you'll find me dreamin'
A country road…
Near the frozen streambeds
A country road…
Don't you want to see
How life…really could be?

In the springtime air
It's a country fair
With the blossoms ablaze
I can smell the breeze
With perfume so sweet
It really can take…
All of my breath away…

Well, I'm a country road…
Can't you hear me callin'
A country road…
Where my words are fallin'
Country road…
Don't you want to feel
How it is to be free?
Well, I'm a country road….
A country road…
A country road…

I'm a Country Road

Believe it or not, I once wrote songs for a rock group in the late seventies. "I'm a Country Road" was one of those poems our group never put to music. However, the singsong type of cadence is so easy to catch onto, it almost sings itself. The poem personifies a road running across the countryside, exploring its identity through the four seasons. Each season presents its own kind of opportunities that the road offers to us as insights and invitations. At the end of each season, the road asks us a question, and each question offers a perspective of where we are on the road of life. Did we live life, or did we watch life pass by like the seasons? Even as a somewhat whimsical poem, there is a serious edge to it.

Trying to pull all this together thematically in a picture was challenging. I could see a laid-back dirt road meandering through the hillsides, passing through the meadows, illustrated with the four seasons, until I tried to sketch it. It wasn't that interesting to do, and the seasons literally piled up upon each other to the point they were indiscriminate. I needed a way to capture the seasons almost like portraits. I did a little study and came up with the idea of creating the ruins of archways where the seasons could be displayed through the openings. My first few sketches looked promising, so I went forward with the larger drawing.

This illustration was started as a pencil sketch and then laid over with dry pastels. Some darker inks were applied at the edges for definition, and then, once the initial background was finished, the foliage and flowers were created. To heighten the colors, I used acrylics both as highlights and shadows. I think the overall effect worked out in the end.

The Forgotten Storm

The Forgotten Storm

I am the forgotten storm
A sea of raging rain…stifled
Thunderous ramparts…unascended
Unseized electric demons…wandering
Veils waiting within carbon clouds…turned violet
I am suspended…seething possibilities.

Impoverished dreams fever intolerance
While darkness unfurls its shabby flag
Over dithering boundaries passionately marked
In rock-hewn walls and concealed lines…
There the Orwellian horses plow unheeded
Wearing humble yokes the privileged endowed
Working the earth horizon to horizon
Keeping the lands free from a field of thorns
While certain unseen specters stay living
In the places marked by unfallowed ground…
I am suspended…

Inscribed upon the emerald backs of leaves
Are the words of mysterious poetry
Only the wisest will ever try to understand…
While mockery inspires uninformed veracities
Kneeling subservient before the Joker's crown
Their defiant words fall in piles of deafening echoes
Salvation broken to heaps now litter the ground…
Raucous tales convert the entangled realities
Clichéd neatly like accepted gospel Trinities
Preached by naïve poets against the door
Inside poisoned temples without a floor…
And I am suspended…

We are the forgotten storm
Our sea of raging rain…growing insidious
Thunderous ramparts awakened…in earsplitting resonance
Unseized electric demons…blinding the firmament
Veils thick with carbon clouds…encroaching the horizon
The storm is coming…
I feel forces pushing inside the changing wind…
I feel fury residing in the lightning's ramparts…
I feel shivering from inside the trembling earth…
I feel strength forged by forgotten words…
I feel the anger cried in tears…
Like raindrops on my skin…

The Forgotten Storm

"The Forgotten Storm" is a poem about controversy and is definitely political in its creation. There are so many lines throughout the poem directly critical of situations created by leaders we entrusted "to do the right thing." One principal concept is immediate as its placement in the poem draws everything to this elemental core of conflict.

> Impoverished dreams fever intolerance
> While darkness unfurls its shabby flag
> Over dithering boundaries passionately marked
> In rock-hewn walls and concealed lines…

"Impoverished dreams" are ideas (hopes) that lost their passion. Dreams without passion are quickly forgotten without hope to sustain them. Dreams as these become dangerous motives ("fever intolerance") to find better dreams beyond the boundaries that contain them. They may begin to follow the "shabby flag" hanging "over dithering boundaries passionately marked, in rock-hewn walls and concealed lines." Dithering boundaries…limits placed without thought to the consequences…passionately marked…those responsible believe zealously and will neither back down nor attempt to compromise. Rock-hewn walls…real tangible borders created with physical markings…concealed lines…borders created that are unseen and often remain unspoken until someone dares to cross them. In insolence, concealed lines are made up (created) when someone speaks out, never knowing such boundaries were created to respond defiantly to any ideas or ideals not acceptable to the aristocracy. It is a "forgotten storm" of consequences with widespread impact.

There is so much more to the poem than this short discussion, but I will leave the rest to your interpretation!

The drawing for "The Forgotten Storm" is equally controversial. First I imagined a field blowing beneath an impending electrical storm. I created this concept with pastels suggesting colors of a wheat field. The colors of this field also needed to resemble a fire, which I did by adding red into the wheat-like colors. In this field, I put man's ruins burning beneath the storm-racked sky. The meaning of the ruins dissembles in the knowledge of what we had (for generations), we could no longer sustain, knowing hope for our future had burned out. In the corner are the Orwellian horses, which, according to George Orwell in his work *Animal Farm*, were the ones responsible for all the hard work. The horses also had the strength to change everything but lacked the knowledge to do it. They were kept ignorant and fiercely believed the truculent rhetoric fed to them. The animals overseeing the farm almost worked the two horses to death, though if the horses could have done it in time, they would have run the perverse leaders off the farm. Opposite the horses are profiles of people with their eyes closed, as if in a dream. When they open their eyes, "the anger cried in tears" will be "like raindrops on my skin." We are all part of "The Forgotten Storm."

Winter Ghost

Winter Ghost

Pull close the gown of winter
Clasps blue-iced like diamond charms
Softly held by fingers weaving
Petaled snowflakes into mantles
Covering crusted fir's naked arms…
Drink in this passionate wind
As thoughts serenely offered
Fill our cut glasses borne from ice
Forged beneath quickened heels
Of a Cossack's swift passage
As he rides into the night…
When the sun spills its last
Over the white-swept hill banks
Listen to its stilled sanguine melodies
Proffered as poured scarlet wine unattended
Played secret memories reposed in harmony…
Bleached faces carved in crevassed stones
Gaze silently across the scattered fields
As ghosts sow their song
Into the snow-filled landscape
Before evening falls
Into the darkest night
Haunted for so long…

Winter Ghost

"Winter Ghost" is a descriptive poem written to describe feelings I had on an early winter's day as I watched the snow drifting against the escaping light of my window about four o'clock in the morning. Written into my forgotten memories of summer were lost promises of light gathering the darkness behind glowing clouds around five o'clock in the morning. However, on this dark December's day, the shadows held their cold grasp without relinquishing any promise of light for several hours. The sense coming from my bleak viewpoint felt haunted, which led me to write "Winter Ghost."

As this is a descriptive poem, it was not difficult to create some of the icons of the poem. I had a lot to work with, almost too much to be honest. The Cossack, the iced-cut goblets, and moodiness of a winter's landscape were features I tried to preserve for the final drawing. The difficulty of this rendering was in the execution of colors needed to create the transparent illusions I needed. My sketchbook, almost filled with designs of other drawings, is now filled with color schemes for this final one.

The final illustration is dominantly dry pastels with a slight application of acrylics. The foreground has the faces of stone watching the progress of winter's ghost as she makes her way through the landscape. I felt I needed to place frozen pine needles into this illustration as it is one of the first visuals in the poem. The other entities portrayed are illustrated to create the remaining atmosphere of "Winter Ghost."

Epilogue

Writing and illustrating *Travelling Through the Ancient Stones* is the creation of decades-long introspection and reflections. These poems were written by a child finding words to express thoughts and feelings, a college student writing about a world filled with injustices and hope, a young man expressing the joys of love and new life, a man later besieged by losses real and imagined, and the old man finding hope and love in his final season. Within these poems are pictures of life, events endowed with great compassion, criticisms of the times that impede living, love, and laughter, controversies affecting the people we care about, and hopefully some of the intense beauty I've experienced and cherished over my time here.

Through the words of poetry, expressions of our feelings bring life into sharp focus. No other medium can paint such deep thoughts in our minds. Poetry exists as a living entity that changes lives and breathes love and hope into our souls. It is alive and lives long after those of us who walked here have travelled through the ancient stones.

Milton Keynes UK
Ingram Content Group UK Ltd.
UKHW020714011223
433473UK00010B/144